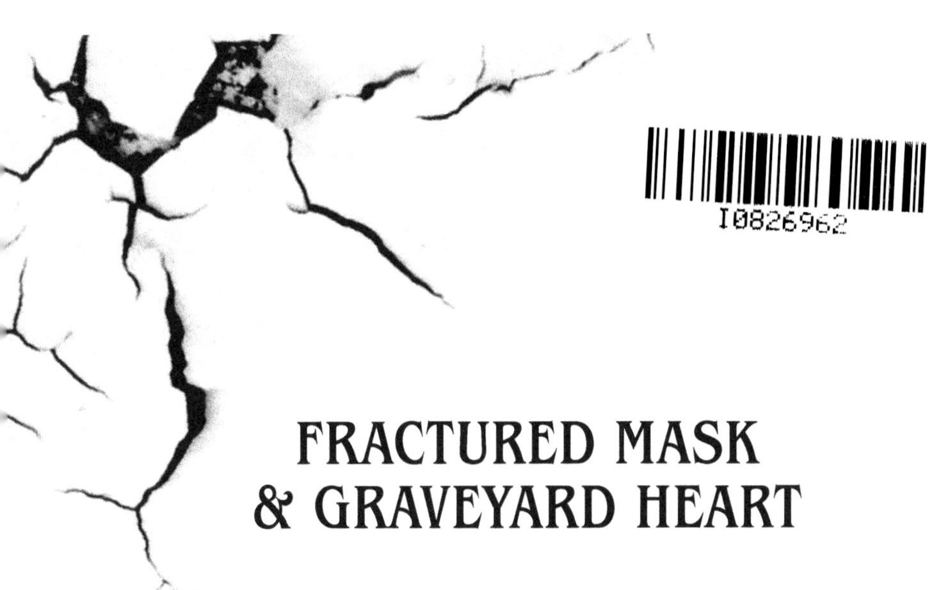

FRACTURED MASK & GRAVEYARD HEART

A POETRY COLLECTION

BECKA ROSE

Fractured Mask & Graveyard Heart

Poetry collection

This book was written entirely by the author without the use of artificial intelligence tools.

Cover art by Cassandra Gordon
Cover design by Becka Rose
Illustrations sketched by Becka Rose
Editing/Proofreading by Alice C.
Interior Book Design by Lisa Michele

ISBN: 978-1-7645913-0-0

ABOUT THIS COLLECTION

This is a gathering of ink bled and threaded together in the process of parentified healing. Here, I have combined words and sketches to bring to life what lives in my mind within this theme.

I resonate with quite macabre themes and used that as inspiration. However, I also found love within myself and with another along the way. This carried a hopeful message for me during a pivotal time, which I wove through these poems.

There are deep roots that have grown from this collection, with many thorns and petals, some fallen and some blooming. These poems flow through seasons as we do in life. From Hopeless depravity, hopeful longevity and everything in between, with the eldest daughter's experience as the stem of this story.

I hope that these words resonate with your soul and help carry your pain as you turn the page.

- Becka Rose

TRIGGER WARNINGS

Self-harm	Depression
Suicidal ideation	Abandonment
Anxiety	Grief

PLAYLIST

Dear reader - Taylor Swift
Messy - Lola Young
Matilda - Harry Styles
Family lines - Conan Gray
Burning down - Alex Warren
Drywall - Paris Paloma
Emails I can't send - Sabrina Carpenter
Older than I am - Lennon Stella
Bones on the beach - Paris Paloma
Nightmare - Halsey
You're on your own kid - Taylor Swift
King - Florence and the Machine
Who's Afraid of Little Old Me - Taylor Swift
Renegade - Big Red Machine ft. Taylor Swift
Savage daughter - Sarah Hester Ross
Don't you see me trying? - Erin LeCount
Vienna - Billy Joel
Audrey Hepburn - Masie Peters
Eldest daughter - Taylor Swift
Call your mom - Noah Kahan
Praying - Kesha
The manuscript - Taylor Swift

For the full playlist scan here!

To the eldest daughters,
Who hurt quietly, heal secluded & hunt for peace,
Keep fighting for your smiles.

TABLE OF CONTENTS

PART THREE

THE HUNTING

"She wields a quill like a sword in the battle with her mind.
The poet, perhaps the most valiant soldier of them all."

Becka-Rose

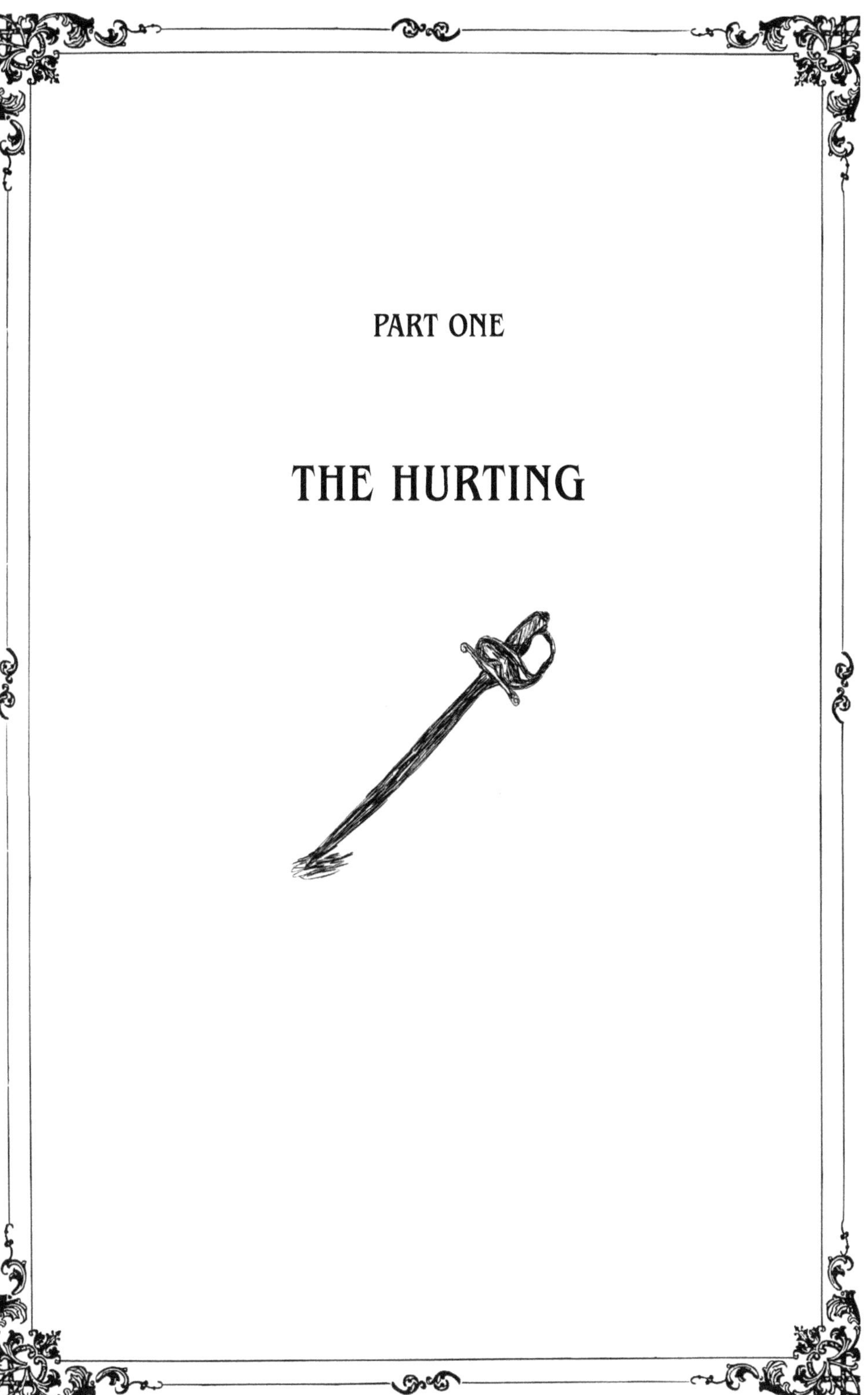

PART ONE

THE HURTING

THE FIRST DRAFT

To be able to rewrite my very first page
Now knowing the horrors that appear with each age

The unrefined prototype
The child where they wing it

A dreaded fate
I gave up trying to escape my locked gate

Learning along the way
When to smile, when to wave
No emotional stability in my wake

The first draft everyone hates
The one that eventually dissipates.

THE
FIRST
DRAFT

SPLENDID PURGATORY

The borrowed fabric of my bones
Inter-woven into our home

To tear my violent hold
Break bones to rebuild the precarious mould

This change ignites cold fear
Reinvention adheres to an infinite dreer

Sickness in saying no
Who am I to leave them alone?

Punishment in the form of dread
Twisted rewards for putting them first again

A nervous system built on toxic empathy:
The eldest daughter's legacy

The imposter syndrome mentality
A meticulously pieced puzzle to reform my personality

Life in splendid purgatory
The beginning, middle, and end of my story.

EXPECT FROM ME

The eldest daughter of doleful three
The deeply rooted crimson tree

Our father left, so I became him next
Of course abandonment was my inheritance

A wolf watching over the pack
The one blamed for every attack

It's easy to be angry
To feel it all and fester madly

To feel my sharp cracks form
Then crumble under the weight of my own walls

I'm easy to hold accountable
Does what you say to me make you feel more powerful?

I know what's said behind my back
Why do you think I brace for an attack?

My empathy equals devastation
Always perceived as easily manipulated

I am different now in every situation
How I used to handle things is severely outdated

You use my cold fire to burn me
Find hope in anticipating the worst of me

My bruised heart beats with the pain
I don't react because I am accustomed to this game.

I will continue to humbly try
Look up at the dancing sky to ask the stars why

To maintain this personality
All because it's what they expect from me.

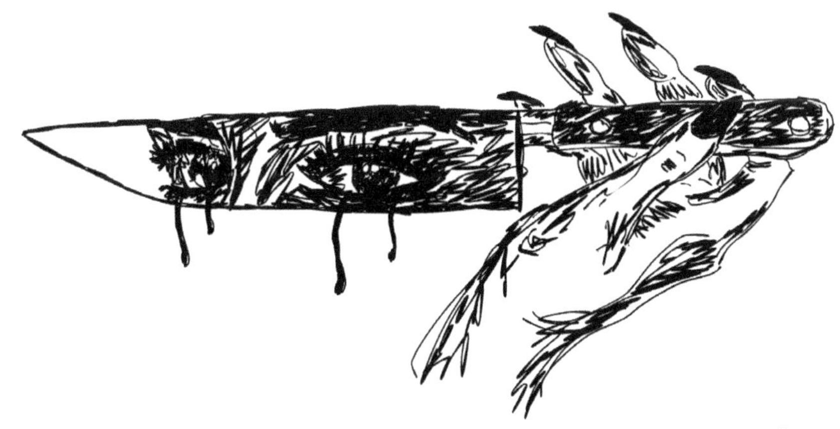

MOTHER FIGURE

From the day I was born
I was her miniature form

My mind required
My time divided

I listen when she cries
Bring smiles into her life

Never the one she will ever have to fight
Her emergency call

The go-to person
A companion through it all

A pretty cage, full of timeless love, innocent manipulation, and a kind heart
A melancholy fate I shall never feel afar.

POISON DAUGHTER

Accelerate the upcoming danger
Savour the taste of pain's sacred flavour

An immunity to selflessness
An addiction to others' helplessness

The hunger for emotional stability
A desire so unfamiliar to me

The sanity-starving act
To keep my family's emotional diet intact

Living in a cauldron
Brewing constant transfigurations

Bittersweet aftertaste
The poison daughter's sharp embrace.

WHEN MY FATHER LEFT

I didn't cry
I didn't frown and ask him why

I lifted my chin
The one I got from him
Despite not knowing what was about to begin

He made his choice
So I raised my cracked voice

He made my mother hide to cry
So I hissed him goodbye

He made my sisters question his care
So I only look at him with my dagger glare

Losing him was not a tragic devastation
Rather, a gruelling confirmation

A home without him has unbroken plaster
Quiet walls and open doors
No reason to run faster

Sharp smile, scary eyes, and screeching soliloquies
What is a man to do when a formidable woman sees through to who he really is?

The only thing of use my father left behind was his shoes
Torn laces, scratchy soles
The ones my younger self stepped into.

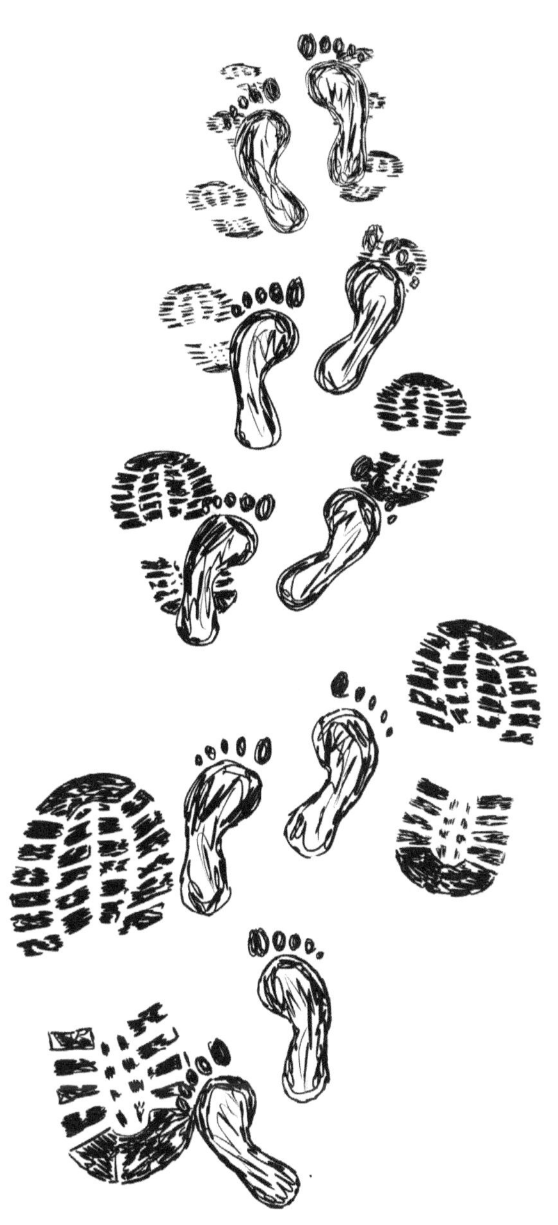

ETERNAL DISAPPOINTMENT

They are watching you through a microscope
Be careful, never true
Stop supplying them with false hope

If they are going to see you cry
Show them how you torturously try

If they grant you emotional access
Give them good advice

If you leave
At the very least, you can visit each week

If you find someone to love
Ensure they know that in your hierarchy, we sit above

If you make plans
Always include them

They are watching you with eternal disappointment
Do not prove them right.

MY FAULT

I found love
It was mine alone
Unaware I would need to atone

I am again reminded that my business is not my own
It's my fault
I didn't know

Privacy is a luxury
I never receive
To ensure formality
I kindly deceive

I attempt to savour my happiness
God forbid they feel unbeknownst

I may have moved out of my home
However, my personal life was never my own.

KARMA'S REPRESENTATIVE

An existence rooted in reliable assistance
The eternal guide for others' lives

Burning torches live in her hands
To light the way for those who are damned

A personified key
A liminal goddess of boundaries

The peacekeeper
Who supplies abundant advice
The one where people go to hide behind

Karma's representative
To pass on evil to those more deserving
The perfect shadow to live in

Protecting homes at all costs
To ensure it is not a place where vile rots

The unarmed guard facing death row
A beam in the night
Standing to take the first and final blow

The leader of her pack
Watchdogs armed at her back

A single woman line of defence
To deflect wickedness is her bequest.

STATUE

I wish I were made of stone
With imperial catacombs to call home

No cracks exposing what's decomposing
Just everlasting granite to keep me safe in i

A carved expression
No need for reinvention

An eternal mood
Formed by sharp tools

To be stared at and judged
Yet no feelings to be smudged

To be a statue
Dispatched from being a scolding shrew.

KINDNESS RETURNED

I held your hand while you stabbed me in the heart
I knew you were hurting, but that's not good enough

I empathised with your pain
Let you stab me over and over again

Your view was valid
Your feelings are real
However, you were cruel
And while I was hurting, I never did that to you

Principles are amins
"We all have different perspectives."

I now don't care that you were hurting
It was my chest you left sliced open

In a perpetual state of no kindness returned
Stitches line my slashed soul
Never to be mourned.

HEAD IN THE SAND

Another dream falling like stones
A freedom privilege I'll never know

To put your head in the sand
Choosing ignorance over resilience
Rather than face life's demands

Too hard to handle
So you candidly cancel

An escape I find permanently unknown
I choose to stay in life's vicious front row

I live on humble reminders
Days filled with putting out fires

I hope your holiday from reality is nice
Let me know what the sand tastes like.

FORGED RAGE

I grew into my formidable cage
Insufferable yet comfortable homage

Their perspective was noxious
The perfect alibi,
An easy excuse for misunderstandings
To the true crime inside my mind

A mother's built-in weapon
Beckoned for emotional stand-ins

A father's fruitful achievement
Until inevitable disappointment

A sibling's authority figure
Responsible for everything wrong with their calibre

Before I learnt to read books, I read moods
Eating my emotions as I entered every room

I am who I am, just as you raised me
Blaming the fierce outcome on how you contained me

A child
I was a child

Grown in a cage that forged my rage.

JEALOUSY'S TOY

My heart started beating
Only to be broken in tandem
Happiness will always be a challenge

Pain and joy can coexist
Both can be consecutively true
Yet only pain was caused by you

Waging a war I never foresaw
A battlefield of carnivorous empathy

The happiest and saddest I have ever been
A rainbow of colliding extremities

No, I wasn't torn when my father left
What you did put me through more distress

Crying behind my back and blaming it on how "You always get mad"
Again, the fault of the angry daughter
If I stand up for myself, it'll prove your point further

They say comparison is the thief of joy
What they don't tell you is that next you become jealousy's toy

The slow dismantling of a twin flame connection
It was always one-sided, until the day I finally decided
Of course you feel abandoned

Whose side are they on?
It definitely wasn't mine, or this sadness wouldn't make me want to
shrivel up and die

If not rooting for my happiness, you ultimately lose
I'm not afraid to be the type of person to choose

I healed without your apology
Now you don't get the same access to me
The ultimate finality

The tribal wound of being hurt by someone you were soul-close to.

BECKA ROSE

SCREAMS CAGED

Tears tucked behind my ear
Smiles adorned with filtered fear

Screams caged behind my ribs
Knots of dread rivulet from my head
With lies woven between chipped lips

Agony echoes in my graveyard heart
Cracked pavement, flickering lanterns
The delusion of a hopeful restart

Strolling past headstones of lost dreams
Trees listen to silent cries as they watch the inked sky
Tearful prayers drawing down aperatic streams

Candles waver in the near distance
Carried down a cold pebbled path with bold resistance
Leading to a mansion of miserable transcendence

Unlocked to corridors of madness
With hidden haunted halls and shadows masking what bites
Where spirits go to cry

A home with a cadence of fears
Where feelings never see the light

My breath is held in the grip of the dead
As a misty breeze silently reaches for my hollowed hand.

RED TEARS

Slaying vampires as placeholders for pain
Trying not to become the demon you hear when they call your name

Condemned to crucify
When all you do is;

Try
Try
Try

A violent fate
A fierce haste
To incinerate who you were

A stern smile
A sharp stare
To deflect those with the audacity to dare

Caging beasts with your will
Only to collapse with the fear of being still

Decorating your persona with an idealised fantasy
An invented alter ego
Confronting the blurred lines of who you are and wish to be

Armed with a sword that never sees the light of day
Something to slay your mental enemies away.

Red tears
Harsh lines
A warrior who's afraid to cry.

DEAR ELDEST DAUGHTER

I can't do anything effortlessly right
Setting off a gruesome combat in my mind

Unable to put up an unprejudiced fight
Barely a glimmer of my blue light

The family psychoanalyst
"You think you're better than us."

The mother figure
"You are not a parent to us."

The distant sister
"You aren't consistent enough."

You try, you fail
You fail, you try

The endless war
A terminal, relentless endure

Be the bigger person
Never get the last word in

Empathy is your twin
Just let them in

Now give them space
You know what it was like at that age.

Your silence is maturity
Responsibility is your shadow

Your tears are second to theirs
It's time you learn how to let things go.

Dear eldest daughter
Don't forget to break the cycle of generational trauma.

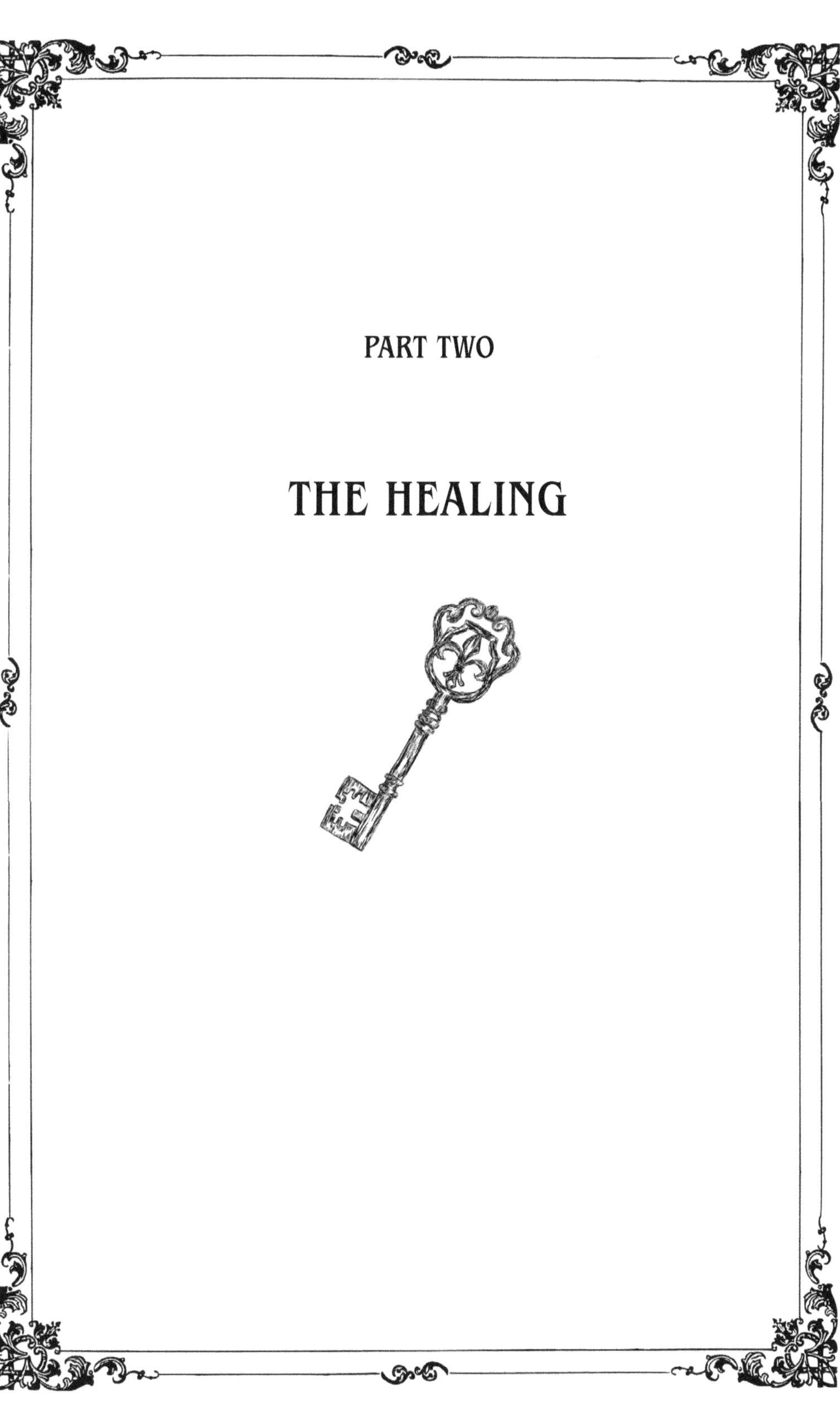

PART TWO

THE HEALING

ETERNAL DISARRAY

Life in layers of ashen paint
A phoenix allergic to the flames

Plucking her feathers to begin again
Trapped within a dark, terror-filled den

Suffocated by her own decay
Inevitable, seething pain
How she makes for easy prey

She is unable to remain the same
And incapable of embarking on change
Welcome home to the clinically insane

So what's the difference between who she is and who she was then?
Long suffering, her dear and terminal friend

For what is a phoenix without her flames?
An insurmountable cycle of eternal disarray.

GLASSHEART

The exstrophy of my heart
A romanticised tendency to pull myself apart

An artificial organ
Rendered to keep hopeful control in

Grief splinters
Betrayal lingers
It burns with expansion, trying to cage my hurt in

Fractures form in the distorted glass wall
Cracks align, which frightens them all

Ruptured splinters grow with each passing day
Tiny shards of woe form with desperate uncertainty

Shattered, not broken
Sharp edges trained to cut those who tear me open

A glassheart
Fragmented mirrors of pains relinquished art.

CACOPHONY OF CHAOS

Raised in a silent summons
A desperate hunger for quiet nothings

Memorising creaky footsteps
Observing empty halls
Resolving everyone's mishaps
Whispering to the walls

Listening out for silent cries
Falling asleep to nightmare lullabies

False narratives
Gaslighting relatives
Planning my demise

Lashing out about how I live my life
When all I can do is;

Survive
Survive
Survive

A house built on bricks of distrust
A home of paper walls and withered love

Who am I without this cacophony?
The comfort in this chaos that has become of me.

I APOLOGISE

For my silenced rage
I could never be myself to your face

I apologise

For being the first to make mistakes in front of them
Before the rules got masterfully rewritten

I apologise

For being so independent
I reject your pointed direction

I apologise

For being so distant
I can't handle being let in

I apologise

For failing to perfectly educate
Never truly knowing my place

I apologise

For I know your intentions were pure
I'm angry about the suffering I endured

I apologise

I'm not running from you
I'm running towards myself.

Finding peace in my truth
The freedom bird for my mental health

I no longer apologise.

SCRATCH & SCREAM

I want to scream
To bite back

I want to hiss
To chalkboard scratch

Force them to hear me
Not to enact the righteous fear they have of me

I am tired of being the bigger person
Yet that's all they can rely on

An identity planted in people pleasing
A pathological meaning

To learn to be gentle
To bottle my screams and cuff my hands
Even as I am hit at every hurdle

"Are you okay?"
Of course
If I weren't there would be unleashed emotional discourse

To seal my pain and mask my hurt
Carrying on the eldest daughter curse

Walking along barbed wire ties
Keeping my truth behind pretty lies and hidden cries.

MATURE

Sharp words, slit souls
She will grow out of it
That's just how it goes

Actions mimic war crimes
A shy, desolate betrayal
I'm sure she didn't mean it this time

Don't say anything, you'll just make it worse
Remember, emotional subterfuge is your curse

You're more self-aware than her
Something you must suffer for

She won't understand your pain
You were different at her age
Don't bother trying to explain

She might one day
When she grows up
One day
When she's mature enough.

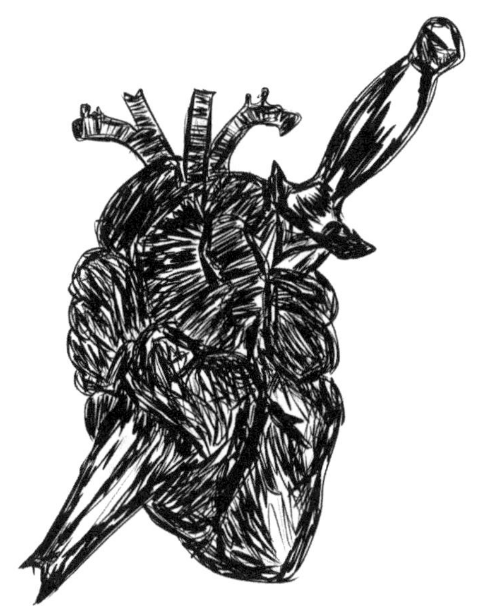

PROPERTY

"That's my sister,
Don't take her from me."
Chasing happiness made me tactless

"She chose a man over us."
Despite my efforts, I feel relentless

To pick and choose the people to please in my life
I never get it right

I choose myself
That screams betrayal

I choose my happiness
The ultimate upheaval

I ask for space
It's thrown back in my face

Cursing the company I keep
All because it's not what they would appoint for me

They tried to save me from a fate that had once been
Wanting the best for me only led down a sanguinary stream

The empaths vow to disembowel anything not aligned
Within the clairvoyance they envisioned for my life

To alter the eldest daughter's prophecy
I must remember I am not my siblings' property.

FAMILY TIES

You handled it so well
Quiet grace
If I didn't, I would have ended up in a stone cell

My truth is trapped behind the bars in my mouth
My eyes tell the story you never beheld

My experience is facing death row
Because it's something you choose not to know

Hiding behind your catatonic lies
Curating a masterful false narrative to live by

My mind screams that it's unfair
Because I don't get to choose to live like I don't care

I'm bitter but decide to be better
I choose ambiguity over ignorance
Even as I fantasise over that disconnected bliss

I can't imagine what it's like to be so pathological that you don't know the difference between your truth and lies

I often wonder if one day you'll wake up to finally see what you did to your family ties.

NO

My first word
A weapon I observed

One I am still learning to use
To sheath my sword
Use my vocal hues

To put myself first using this word
Rather than please those who demand to be heard

No, I don't want to
No, I shouldn't have to
No
No
No.

A word in my pocket I never use
A habit formed from nurture
Something most people love to abuse

A word that carries the weight of my existence
A venomous, addictive desistance.

GOOD PERSON

Protect your peace
Put your mind at ease

Set firm boundaries
It's not the paradox that it seems

Be righteously selfish
What do you need?

You're not the enemy despite leaving home
I know the rue weighs like a 2-ton stone

They need you
You need to breathe more
It's time you closed that antiquated door

You'll drown before you do it again
In your freedom there's no mask to mend

Cold silence you don't have to seek
No footsteps to listen out for while you sleep

You're still a good person despite your guilty smile
It's the first real one you've had in quite a while.

FEATHERED FOOTPRINTS

I held my shaking breath
As I closed the unlocked door and left

Forcing myself not to look back
Despite the heaving anxiety attack

Faultered hesitancy
A creeping realisation of what independence could be

I stepped on the crack
Breaking something more
So I often looked back
Every day, my heart felt chronically sore

I saw the damage on my exit
The glue of the family has gone raw

And yet…

A smooth, crisp breeze
Feeling a smile slip through my teeth

Quiet nights
A routine revolving around myself
No terrors to fight
A new sense of self

Feathered footprints into a euphoric life
Where the only torture left is in my mind.

WHEN I GROW UP

A tenacious gap I must secure
No longer trying to instinctively conceal

To bring peace to my life
Rather than feel like I need to hide

I will become evermore
Shifting my smiles to the sky
Not attempt to erase myself raw

To heal these pains
I will overthrow the generational chains

I will be assuredly myself
Find strength in asking for help

An ease unlike one I have ever felt
No longer restrained by the fear of becoming the cards I was dealt.

CONFESS

She's the Gothic Cathedral
Where people go to lay down regrets
The theatre girl gone regal

Where everyone can freely speak behind her carved doors
She removes scarred troubles from their haunted halls

Knowing they will always be listened to
Given advice and told they'll be alright
A feeling she is addictively accustomed to

That's her fate
A beautiful building that holds everyone's guilt

Embellished with seats for everyone to take
A sacred, whispered space

Stained glass windows to stow away from the world
The truth of a cathedral built girl

The third parent without the sense to run
The sibling so serious she's no longer fun

Her purpose is her life experience
Not that she has much to give

But she will always be there for your text
"Hey, I have something to confess."

SOMETHING TO PROVE

Their pain is tattooed on my skin
A daily reminder of the body I am trapped in

What once felt playful
Is now disgraceful

Salvation in my isolation
A sanctuary to bear my suppression

Safely rooted behind closed doors
Nobody can witness the horrors I have caused

Gloves to hide the shaking
Fake smiles don't show what's always been breaking

Hair woven into a crown
A fake impression
Never let them down

An empty ice castle
Cold and sharp reflections
My feelings always cause a startle

The perfect hiding place to cry in
Where my veracity is not worth denying

No more concealing hard truths
Maybe one day
I won't have something to prove.

WITCH ON THE RUN

Do you have what it takes to be caged?

To remain principled and quiet
Cast aside your emotional damage

To act centre stage
Their script tells you what to say

Cynacisum in command
Abrasive comebacks rot calmly in my hand

The cracked mask of oppression
A deeply rooted clinical depression

Living a secretive life
One I also can't seem to get right

An infinite sacrifice
Would they just be better off if I died?

Always fighting for what I believe in
Yet never caring how I am treated

A younger sibling suffering from comparison
How they'll never know the half of it

I am the wicked that this way comes
The name of the witch, despite her goodness
Still needs to run.

GRAVEYARD HEART

Corpse candles line the sombre way
Floating through the headstones of dismay

Shadowed silhouettes weave between bone trees
Wilted flowers are buried with the dead who catch fallen leaves

Carved names, arched stone
Dreams unanswered, loneliness atoned

A misty yard of hopeless eternity
Knitting spirals of terminal depravity

The reaper's home
A poisoned pulse
A dismal heirloom to bestow

A soul with immunity to decay
An apparition dressed in esoteric misery

Wearing a shredded shadow like a coat of lost hope
Thoughts are a smoky hood covering her mind as a comforting ghost would

In her hand, a candelabra carries screams
Burning wax dances down her skin, reminding her she can't breathe

The girl with a graveyard heart.

FRACTURED MASK

A lobotomized expression
The silicon smile succession

The weight of unbidden frowns
Nothing compares to my bloody crown

I smile through tears
Disorientating my fears
My favoured empirical discretion

Every smile cracks the stone armour
Each wrinkle disarms the hardened plaster

For what better to interfere with my macabre facade
Then a fractured mask to expose my graveyard heart.

UNRELIABLE NARRATOR

I am an open book with words in a secret language
Feel free to turn the page
Only I control what you imagine

You think you know me
That's how I make it seem

I had grown into my mask
Wore it every day like fine art

The stitches of who I was have come undone
Who have I become?

This narrator is unreliable
Chapters unravelled
The reader is in constant denial

Close this book
See my truth
Stop asking *"what happened to you?"*

No longer distorting what you read
My mask is off
I set myself free
Now you need to start again in getting to know me.

PART THREE

THE HUNTING

EMOTIONAL EXILE

I grew thorns in place of flowers
Learnt alone to conquer my powers

Never the angel my sibling could be
But ever the witch, they shan't achieve

My life in emotional exile
Stunted since I was a querulous child

A panther caged
Always told I needed to be tamed

Flora and fauna for family
Finding home engulfed amongst ghost trees

A voice of enchantment
With a cauldron brewing poisonous weapons

A life away from human interaction
Something I never had much luck with

Immense cryptic power
Endless enemies to devour

How minacious a sorceress without more to lose
The savage daughter with infinite options of who
she can change into.

MISINTERPRETED HEALING

Did I heal?
Or was I just used to the pain?
Was this my desperate excuse to get through each day?

A delusion to eradicate the eloquent intrusion
A way to pardon the emotions I kept at bay

Given the thistled crown
A coronation of damnation
Wearing an upside-down frown

The diligent but wishingly wild inner child
Hiding behind a robe of silence and a saviour complex gone quiet

The actor with a tired identity
Who favours broken mirrors and paper splinters
Glamourising solidarity

I know exactly why I am like this
Who I am is no existential question
The real question is, how do I be different?

Days start crumbling under the weight of these tasks
Nights end with falling apart when I crawl home and unstitch the intricate mask

Now I see the problem wasn't always me
I needed to make a drastic change
Not attempt to decimate my burning pain

The poet, forced to be a king
Their leader, always problem-solving
Is finally able to lyrically unpack her misinterpreted healing.

PLEASANT DECEIVING

An identity formed from the slivered cracks in stone walls
Carrying myself on eggshell floors

The eldest daughter syndrome is the only home I know
Finding solace in fixing what breaks
Helping people stitch up their mistakes

The gifted child
Not the girl gone wild

The one so mature for her age
Who is so earnest that she locks the door to her own cage

The old soul
The daughter of decorum
Who you never lose control of

None of this is a complaint
I wouldn't have it any other way

I live for being needed
Find purpose in people- pleasing

I'm elated that this role was chosen for me
Even on the days my grief feels heavy

For there isn't someone I'd rather be
Than the girl with an identity rooted in pleasant deceiving.

GRIM FAMILY

Desperation for a familial unit
Is the number one cause of why you'll lose it

A daughter desperate for autonomy
A mother who is afraid of what this could mean.

One and the same
Both are the black sheep of their families

A defiance in coexistence
A longing for consanguine independence

I do not tolerate relationships based on blood bonds
There is something wrong with unconditionally trusting those
I share DNA from

I am not my family
I wish upon every fallen star for sole custody of me

My distance isn't disrespect
What's wrong with being ambivalent?

We share the same Gothic architecture
Yet universally different shades of behaviour

I learnt from your devastating mistakes
Don't curse me for what I chose to change

A family akin to a corrupt government
Something I will always stand up against

Challenging authority
Knowing there is so much more I could be
Than the eldest daughter of a grim family

UNCONDITIONAL TOLERANCE

A conversation with blank eyes
Using tears in place of words.
Why do I even try?

Blood is thicker than water
It's much easier to choke on
A red stain on white clothes

A stench I can't remove
The UV light shows invisible lines
Something I can't prove

The unconditional love of a family
An easy excuse to tolerate toxicity

A chronic skin stain
Carrying the family like terminal back pain

The people I can never let down
(even though I always do)
Gasping when I have a tilted crown

What happens when they leave you?
The tolerance was a lonely existence
Your behaviour is not something they intended to remain akin to

The loophole of a close family dynamic keeps you untuned
The belief that this is not something you could lose
Oh, how that turned out to be untrue

The staples of patience are unravelling
The desire to stay away is vastly more fascinating

The stab wounds of sharp words
Hold infections from kindness misused

The love I have for you is unconditional, true loyalty
However, the tolerance is beyond capacity
This is why you had to be removed from my story

THE DIFFERENCE BETWEEN US

Should I just tell you how it is?
Or would that cause more carnage?

I kept my hurt in my pocket
How you treated me, tucked in my chained locket

Every breath I take suffocates
But between the two of us, I have what it takes

To dish it out, not able to take it back
If I told you, you'd be a dysregulated mess
No wonder you have anxiety attacks

You're not the only one with big feelings
Others choose the route of intentional healing

Is it that I am intimidating, or does my presence make your conscience quake?
Self-aware of your ignorance
Continuing to choose lazy bliss

Missiles fired of self-righteousness
The desolation of kinship

If it were up to me, I'd pick your teeth
Pulling out the weeds that prohibit your vocabulary

No, it's not that you're a bitch
It's that you're solely nonchalant
A frivolous covert narcissist in fancy font.

That's what I'd say if I could tell you how it is
Too bad kindness is my kin
I'd rather keep it in than continue your hurting

Is that healthy?
Probably not
Your healing is not my chore
I'm too tired
My loyalty feels raw
I'm now not afraid to close the armoured door

That's the difference between those who hurt and hurt back
To those who hurt and choose to heal rather than attack

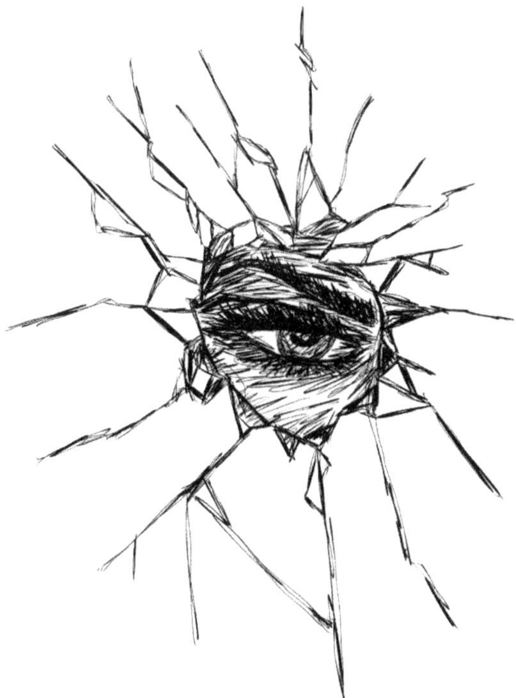

PEACE IS MY REBELLION

I didn't choose to host these wounds
Yet it's my choice to heal what you didn't want to

No longer tolerating what you benefit from
Your peace is not my job

Catering to my invisible scares
Weaving stitches like making patterns with stars

Boundaries of recovery
What was once a wishful fantasy

A guilty conscience
Crafted from a conditioning of everlasting caution

Sacrificing habits
No longer posing as an emotional captive

Becoming someone I met in a dream
Peace is my rebellion.

VIRGINIA CREEPERS

The quiet is now calm
There's no need to feel triggered or alarmed

My Elizabethan walls feel like a home
A place where I'm not defiantly alone

An aspiration I had years in the making
Something I made whilst my heart was breaking

Freedom akin to folklore
Dreams live behind whimsical fairy doors

Watching Virginia creepers climb my stone walls
Renovating my prison into evergreen halls

A place for snow to sit
Where butterflies cocoon and patiently bloom
A stability throughout seasons and a timeless felicity

A sanctuary at my will
To know I can be gracious
To let my mind be still.

INNER CHILD

She was fifteen at twelve
Felt things most her age were never dealt

She was a ferocious child
What happened to her blue fire?

Sticks in her unkept hair
She never seemed to care
Where is all her ire?

She was twenty at sixteen
Her ambitions were just a vast daydream

To be reckless, careless, throw back your head and
Say to hell with all of it

She had to provide
It was her way to survive

Now at twenty-five
Her inner child cannot hide

She's peeking through the fragmented cracks
Hearing hope breathe when she laughs

Discovering what it's like to be selfish
An unfamiliar yet desired form of wealthy

She's silly, cancels plans, says she doesn't give a shit
No more trying to be older than she is

PERMISSION

I give myself permission to venture into the unfamiliar
As I choose to be the trailblazer

The comfort in that chaos was my preferred predictable home
What could happen if I choose to toss this heavy stone?

A first step into discomfort
Screams echo
A family unravelling because I left

Another step closer to peace
Even as I feel like a withering autumn leaf

I give myself permission to feel this pain
I know it'll become a distant memory

It's okay to feel guilty
What's not is letting it sway you off your pathway

Soon, the echoes sound like waves praising your name
You've reached the shores of your pain

The sand between your feet is the endless hope of prosperity

The warm sun smiles on your troubled skin stain
Reminding you that your life is only ever yours to live
Hear revival in your name

The multi-coloured blue waves symbolise how one thing is never always quite the same
How you can transform as the ocean does
And you smile because that's what you've always done

Give yourself permission.

REFLECTION

I saw my old self in the mirror

She didn't think I'd be here
I thought my reflection would run away

Her hair is messy and loud
Mine is natural and proud

She wears baggy black clothes
Suffocating a starved body whilst hiding behind dark makeup

I wear a black sundress
Showing a newfound health with my face fresh from rest

She raises a brow
I smirk

She asks if our vision is worse
I tell her we wear a low vision badge at work

She looks defeated
I feel determined

She covers her wrists in her sleeves
I show her our scars now breathe

We both tilt our heads
Observing

She asks what we do now
I say heal our inner child

She smiles, which is rare
I smile back, seeing the tears there

She asks about our family
I imply broken but mending

I tell her we are free, travelling the world
Our voice rattling the trees
Creativity and resolve being our key

We say goodbye
Knowing it'll be a while
She gifts me one last rare, sad smile.

THE ELDEST SON

Strong hands and kind eyes
Saw me at my worst and kept sending warm smiles

Hidden stares and mesmerising smirks
Always knew how to take my mind off what hurt

He held me when I fell
Knew who to call and what would help

A stranger who saw me for who I am, not my potential
A man who took me as I was and couldn't be more gentle

A man quietly obsessed
Even as I feign disinterest

I was scared my mental health would put him off
Something I often lost control of

Nothing was deterring
Even as my haunted world cursed him

He held my heart through the cyclone
Saying he would never leave me to weather storms alone

"My mind is a dark place too, but now it's consumed by you."

The eldest son of a healthy home
The heart that beats rhythmically with my own.

LOVE ANOMALY

Something rare
Simply divine

A love that stirred passion
Subtly sublime

A force unparalleled for my favoured discourse
A fate I didn't think I would be ordained for

A love I thought existed exclusively in fiction
You showed me this was something I could believe in

Once convinced, men were only capable of being walking red flags
Or manipulative and abusive dads

Before you came along
I was the toughest man I've ever known

Turning my parentified mind
Into a passenger princess state of pride

You altered my ruinous prophecy
Proving you are my love anomaly.

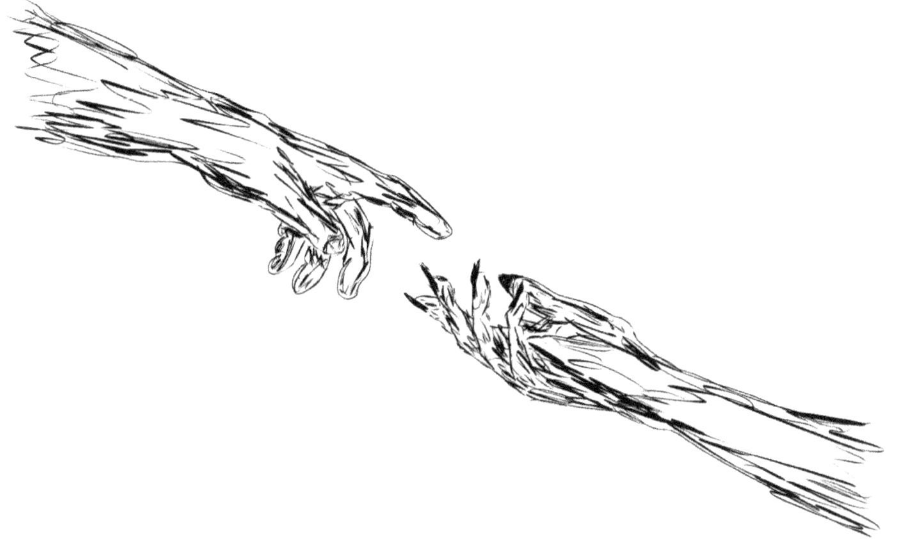

VERSIONS OF ME

I am the most me I have ever been
Separating myself from old responsibilities

Not a reinvention
A self-discovery from hindered discretion

Simply just the daughter
An identity I've always fought for

I accept my femininity
Found comfort in my softness
No longer just a daydream

I'm not a scary scrutineer
Or an emotionally detached scoundrel
Seeing myself through your eyes is a crucial surprise

My sharp nails are now periwinkle
Shimmering like your irises
My very own daylight crystals

You love every version of me
Helped me see ones I never thought I could be.

MY DUTY

With him, I lay down my worn sword
I take off my charred armour
I break the barbed wards.

There is safety in his strong embrace
Sacred time spent with just the two of us

I cherish our rituals of joy
When love is easy
A quiet remedy

I feel light, free, and at ease
My salvation where emotions never freeze

There is a radiance when I am relaxed
No room for devious anxiety attacks

His affirmations are my revelations
Approval to be soft and childlike
An invitation where freedom feels like a shrike

Dancing in the kitchen
Living roles we can play reverse in

Singing to me in the car
Survival mode, I can disarm

Telling him about the books I read
Listening when he tells me history's feats

My life is more than my duty
Where childhood can extend till we are over fifty

He looks at life with wonder
Wanting to cherish every moment with me and ponder

Life with him is an adventure every day
The safest I've felt and my preferred ecstasy

Our home is not a battle where I need to retaliate
It is a place where rest is something to celebrate.

RESURRECTED

Counteracting my curse
My dark cloud is now a mist of old hurt

Lifting my iniquitous spell
Carrying my soul back from my curated hell

A dark abyss became a place I called home
Somewhere, I hope my future will never know

You walk through my graveyard with my heart in your hand
Clearing cobwebs
Getting to know the map of my eerie land

Guarding my threaded back
I no longer need to brace for an attack

Knocking on my deadbolt doors
Picked up my shattered glass
Moped the tear-soaked floors

It's always been you
Right from the start
From the moment when you resurrected my graveyard heart.

AUTOPSY

A cold table
A ruptured muse
A skin coffin in stagnant use

A body without a burning purpose
What used to be a concealed furnace

A land mine bloodstream
A stomach of empty tombstones
Bone fabric threaded from muscle memories

A glassheart graveyard with headstones of dreams
Broken ribs echo reckless screams

Chipped lips that weaved lies into lullabies
Hallowed eyes reflected a girl much older than she was
Unseeing irises that saw through to shrivelled souls

Her heart, a sponge that combusted trying to hold it all inside
She no longer needs to;

Try
Cry
Try

Cracked hands that held the love and loss of her family
Curled hair in knots of dread
A throat enclosed from toxic empathy

Spider-webbed scars of uncertainty line her wrists
From a time when she didn't have life ambition

Red tears drip from where she was holding thorns
Stone shoulders crumbled from the weight of it all

Wrinkles aligned from guilty smiles
Teeth chipped from words kept in
Burnt skin from her blue fire

Feet cut from eggshell floors
Nails torn from scratching chalkboard walls

Tear streams of relief constellate her cheeks
A soul that can now feel at peace

The autopsy of an eldest daughter.

THE END

ACKNOWLEDGMENTS

To my love Sam, I couldn't be more appreciative for your unconditional support. You have always believed in my art and that it deserved to be seen. Thank you for pushing me, always asking how it's going, and holding me accountable.

To my family, for the good and the bad. Without either, this book wouldn't be what it is, and I wouldn't be who I am. Especially my mother, who as an eldest daughter, was one of my muses.

To my best friend Lauren, the first person I shared this book with, and who helped me immensely. Your support and belief in this book pushed me further to chase this dream.

Cass…where do I start? Thank you for always being a shoulder for me to lean on. Your positivity and care have carried me through so much. Your excitement and passion for this collection have lifted my spirits. You brought to life the cover with your own elegant art, and I am so grateful I got to share this passion project with you.

To Alice, thank you endlessly for your sharp eye and editing skills! Typos and errors would be abundant without you!

To Lisa, who guided me from the formatting stage all the way to publication and marketing! You are a beaming star, and I am so grateful for you!

To my Alpha readers: Ellen, Alice, Lauren, Cass, Jess & Rosie. I am thankful for your help in reviewing this collection before it was released to the world and for being so supportive of me along the entire way! To Sawyer and Theodore - my two fur babies, who made for the best writing companions.

To my ARC readers, I truly appreciate you saying yes to reading and sharing the love for my book! It honestly means more than words.

To you - the reader, who picked up this book and took the time to read each page, thank you, thank you, thank you! I appreciate your support immensely.

Also, a massive thank you to my psychologist - Katie, who, over the past ten years, has heard it all and helped me navigate what I have written here, as well as much more. Writing was never a healthy outlet for me until I truly found my voice and learnt to wield my pen in a way that captured what I needed to say.

ABOUT THE AUTHOR

Becka Rose is 26 and lives in QLD, Australia, with her partner Sam & 2 cats - Sawyer (soy bean) & Theodore (Theo). She has a few novels in the making, including more poetry and will be publishing in the years to come. When she isn't writing, she is reading, attending bookish events to support her fellow Authors or travelling. One of her favourite places in the world is the Welsh countryside.

To keep up with her writing & travels, follow along on her socials:

Instagram: @ beckarose.author
Tik tok: @ beckarose.books & @ beckarose.author
Youtube: @ becka.bookss
Email: beckaroseauthor@gmail.com

I would be honoured if you could please review on Amazon, Goodreads &/or social media! Reviews mean so much to authors & I would be eternally grateful!

www.ingramcontent.com/pod-product-compliance
Lightning Source LLC
LaVergne TN
LVHW010625100826
845148LV00014B/3118
9781764591317